Me and My Horse

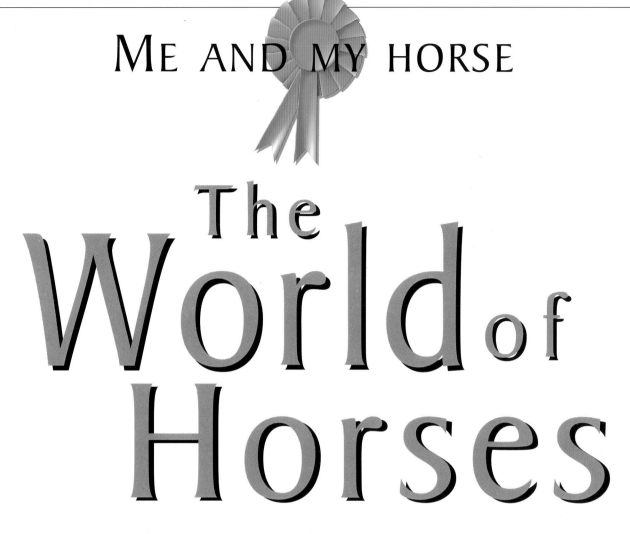

The World of Horses

Toni Webber

COPPER BEECH BOOKS
Brookfield, Connecticut

© Aladdin Books Ltd 2002

Produced by:
Aladdin Books Ltd
28 Percy Street
London W1T 2BZ

ISBN 0–7613–2852–1

First published in the United States in 2002 by:
Copper Beech Books,
an imprint of
The Millbrook Press
2 Old New Milford Road
Brookfield, Connecticut 06804

Editor:
Harriet Brown

Designers:
Flick, Book Design & Graphics
Simon Morse

Picture researcher:
Brian Hunter Smart

Illustrators:
Peter Barrett, McRae Books—Italy,
David Burroughs, Donald Harley—
BL Kearley, Angus McBride, Simon
Morse, Richard Orr,
Francis Phillipps, Rob Shone,
Stephen Sweet—SGA

Cartoons: Simon Morse

Certain illustrations have
appeared in earlier books
created by Aladdin Books.

Printed in U.A.E.

Cataloging-in-Publication data is on
file at the Library of Congress.

10 9 8 7 6 5 4 3 2 1

Contents

Introduction

The World of Horses is a lively guide to horses from every corner of the globe. Horses have evolved over millions of years to give the creatures that we know and love today. Over the years, horses have had many different uses—from farming to racing, war to delivering messages. In some parts of the world they are still used as work animals, but elsewhere they are mainly used in sports and in leisure time.

There is so much to find out about horses. I'll have to write it all in my diary —that should help me to remember!

Did you know?

Look in these boxes for further information about the fascinating world of horses. They contain surprising facts about horses from all over the world.

Q What are these boxes for?

A These question and answer panels are here to help answer your questions about horses. Each panel is relevant to the subject on the rest of the page. Find out how many different breeds there are in the world or how big the first horses were. Learn about mythical horses and find out when stirrups were first invented and why they are so useful.

Monday
I didn't want to go to school today. I was in the middle of rereading one of my favorite pony books. It's about a girl who owns a horse on a ranch. One day I'm going to go to the Wild West and have my own Western horse!

The horse family

Horses have been used for riding, hauling goods, and farm work in many parts of the world. Different types have been bred for different uses. Today, the tiny Shetland pony and the huge workhorse look very different, yet they both have a common ancestor.

ARABIAN

Perhaps the most beautiful horse of all time, the Arabian is noted for its concave face, glorious head, and high tail carriage. It displays amazing stamina and extreme hardiness. It is a native of the Middle East and is used for all types of work from riding and racing, to pulling carts and carrying produce. The true Arabian is not very big. It stands at between only 14.2 and 15 hands high (57 to 60 inches), but it is a unique horse.

RUSSIAN GOLDEN HORSE

The narrow Russian horse, the Akhal-Teke, is known as the "golden horse." This is because it has a bright, metallic golden sheen on its coat. Originally a desert horse, it is thought to be an ancestor of the Arabian. It has great speed and stamina.

Morning
I wish I knew exactly what breed of pony Oscar is. I expect he's a crossbreed, but he doesn't have a pedigree so I can't be sure.

Did you know?

There are about 300 different horse and pony breeds in the world. They range from the heavy horses of northern Europe to the tiny Falabella pony of South America. One original wild horse, the Tarpan, still exists in captivity. But Przewalski's horse, discovered in Mongolia in the 1920s, is now thought to be extinct. Both of these original wild horses display coarse, heavy heads, a stand-up mane, and a dorsal stripe.

HANOVERIAN

Originally bred in Germany, the Hanoverian was used for riding and farmwork. It was later crossed with thoroughbreds to produce a well-built riding horse. Many leading European riders ride Hanoverians, and these horses are very much in demand for show jumping.

IRISH HUNTER

The Irish hunter is not a breed but a type. Ireland produces some of the finest horses in the world. The Irish draft horse is a strong, well-built working horse. As horses were used less in agriculture, the Irish draft was crossed with the thoroughbred to produce a riding horse. This was then bred with Connemara horses to become the popular Irish hunter.

Shetland pony
Scotland

NATIVE PONIES

Of all the regions in the world, the British Isles have the largest number of different breeds of native pony—nine in total. The New Forest and Welsh ponies are ideal for children to ride. Scandinavia and Iceland also have small, hardy native ponies, all of them strong enough to carry grown-ups.

New Forest pony
England

Exmoor pony
England

Thursday
I am keeping a scrapbook of all the horse breeds of the world —with a difference. I can put a picture of any breed in, but only if I have actually seen it. So my book isn't coming along very fast! I told Mom that a tour of Russia would be a good idea, followed by a trip around Scandinavia, but you can guess what she said.

Q Are horse fairs still held?

A Horse fairs—places where horses and ponies are bought and sold—still exist, such as Golega Fair in Portugal, below. In England, one of the best known is the Stow Fair in Gloucestershire, where young ponies can be bought quite cheaply. The pony breed societies hold annual sales of yearlings that can be trained to become good riding ponies. The sales help control the numbers of wild ponies roaming their natural habitat.

Across continents

Sunday
There are two kinds of pinto horses, the Ovaro and the Tobiano. The Ovaro is dark with patches of white over it. The Tobiano has a white coat with large patches of dark color. Pintos were popular with Native Americans and cowboys.

Today, wherever you go in the world, the primary use of horses and ponies is for recreation. In some poor countries the horse still fills its traditional role—that of helping its master to make a living. But the bond between horse and master may still be very close.

SOUTH AMERICA

This is the home of horses descended from Spanish horses imported nearly 500 years ago. The Argentinians ride Criollos. These are short, stocky horses that are well suited to herding cattle. Criollos are crossed with thoroughbreds to make very good polo ponies. Argentina is also home to the smallest pony in the world—the Falabella. This tiny pony stands at less than 7 hands (28 inches) high.

ASIA

Remains of prehistoric horses have been found in India, and horses are said to have been introduced into China 4,000 years ago. The Chinese pony is very similar to the Mongolian pony, which resembles the early Tarpan horse (page 4).

AUSTRALIA

There are no horses native to Australia. The Waler, now an Australian breed, is descended from horses brought by settlers in the 1700s. Brumbies, wild horses living in the outback, come from horses turned loose in the gold rushes of the 1800s.

Waler
Australia

CONQUISTADORS

The Spanish who discovered and conquered the New World, the conquistadors, brought their horses with them. These caused as much interest, awe, and excitement among the native Americans as did the arrival of the white men themselves. Until this time, the American continent had no horses at all. Some escaped into the wild, and were the ancestors of the wild horses of the plains.

Appaloosa
U.S.

Pinto
U.S.

NORTH AMERICAN HORSES

The American quarter horse, with its short bursts of speed and ability to turn and twist, is ideally suited to cattle-herding. The remarkable Tennessee walking horse, with its amazingly comfortable running gait, suited the plantation owner's need to spend all day in the saddle without getting tired.

Tennessee Walking Horse
U.S.

MUSTANGS

The wild horse of America, the mustang, is a direct descendant of the horses that came over with the Spanish conquistadors. Big herds of these horses used to roam the plains of the central U.S. but they were long considered worthless. So, fifty years ago, a registry of Spanish mustang horses was established with the aim of preserving their best characteristics —hardiness, intelligence, and stamina.

The Western horse

In the American West, the horse had a particular function—herding cattle across the vast plains of the continent and carrying its rider many miles a day. No wonder that the Western horse displays special characteristics and wears a saddle and bridle well suited to its role in life.

Later—I'm in big trouble. I took Oscar's noseband off to turn him into a cowboy horse and now I've lost it. I was sure I'd left it in the tack room. Now I've got to use my allowance to buy a new one. Still, he really looked like a Western horse!

RODEO
Rodeo competitions provided cowboys with a chance to show off their riding and cattle skills. Today they are a popular attraction in the American West. They offer prizes to riders who can stay on a bucking horse the longest, rope a calf the quickest, and ride a bull without falling off.

JUNIOR RODEO RIDERS
America has an association of young rodeo riders. Their ages range from under-8 to 19, and they compete at all sorts of cowboy contests. Rodeos include goat tying, calf roping, steer wrestling and riding, bareback riding, and bronco riding.

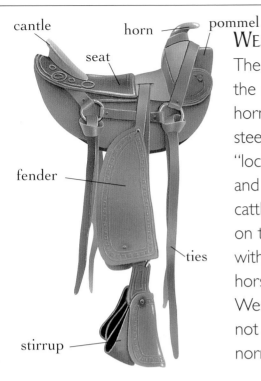

cantle   horn   pommel

seat

fender

ties

stirrup

WESTERN SADDLE AND BRIDLE

The seat of the Western saddle is deep, for the comfort of the rider on a long ride. The horn is for attaching a rope when roping steers. The cantle and pommel are high to "lock" the rider in position when twisting and turning during the process of herding cattle. The Western bridle has long shanks on the bit that are used in conjunction with a leather curb strap to act on the horse's poll (the part of the head between the ears). Western bridles don't have a noseband. Split reins—reins not buckled together—are popular. One-handed riding is normal, so cowboys steer their horses using neck-reining.

MYTHS AND MODERN WAYS

Cowboys did spend many hours in the saddle and they slept under the stars. But they did not ride the huge horses that you see in Western films. Real cowboys preferred small horses, often ponies, and usually rode more than one a day. Cowboys sometimes changed mounts six times a day. Today, cowboys are more likely to be seen on dirt bikes or at rodeos than out on a horse.

Annabel and I tried roping a fence post, and the loop never came near enough. Just imagine trying it with a moving steer!

WESTERN TRAILS

The modern-day rider can enjoy a great vacation at a Western ranch catering to tourists, riding out on the old cowboy trails. Trail rides can be just one day or you can go on longer rides lasting several days. Accommodation usually involves camping out at night and cooking your own food on an open fire. Trail riding is enjoyed by many people.

Racehorses

From the time when horses were first domesticated, riders have tried to outdo each other. Racing has existed as an organized sport for about 400 years. Today it is done worldwide. The best horses are greatly admired and can be worth a great deal of money.

THOROUGHBRED

The thoroughbred is the fastest horse in the world. It is descended from one of three Arabian stallions, the Darley Arabian, the Byerley Turk, and the Godolphin Barb. Every racehorse entered in the General Stud Book has at least one in its pedigree. The thoroughbred develops early. This is why two-year-olds can be ridden and raced. Every thoroughbred's official birthday is January 1st.

WHERE IT ALL BEGAN

The ancient Greeks enjoyed public racing, but in much of Europe for the next thousand years or so, racing was mainly private. In the late 1600s, it became more formalized in England, and other countries soon followed suit. The Jockey Club was created to oversee the sport.

STEEPLECHASING

Racing over jumps used to be held between two landmarks, often the steeples of churches (hence steeplechasing). The world's most famous race over jumps—the Grand National—began in 1839. Most horses in jump racing today start by racing on the flat. Too slow for flat racing, they are tried over hurdles, then over jumps. If the longer distance suits them, they can race for many more years.

RACING AROUND THE WORLD

There are several great races. Among the most famous are the English Derby, the American Kentucky Derby, the Australian Melbourne Cup, and the French Prix de l'Arc de Triomphe. Race meetings are held all over the world and provide a focal point of interest for local people. Hong Kong's racetrack, Happy Valley, is set in the middle of the crowded city.

The English Derby, run at Epsom
England

Happy Valley Racetrack
Hong Kong

The Kentucky Derby, Churchill Downs, *Kentucky*

Friday
I really would like to be a jockey. Girls and boys can be apprenticed to racehorse trainers now. But Dad says it's a hard life and only the very best can get to the top. Perhaps, one day, I could be the very first girl to win the Kentucky Derby!

TROTTERS

Harness-racing is popular in America and France. The horses have been trained to move at an amazingly swift trot instead of a gallop. Their other artificial gait, the pace, is where the legs on the same side move forward at the same time. These two gaits ensure the horse pulls the two-wheeled, lightweight sulky very smoothly.

Riding styles

Through the ages, most riding styles have changed. A few have stayed much the same as always. Others have been affected by clothing styles, social attitudes, or improvements in technique. In some cases, the interest of modern-day enthusiasts keeps an older riding style going.

3 pm—I tried riding like a medieval knight on Oscar the other day. They used to ride with really long stirrups. It wasn't very easy, especially when it came to rising trot. It's almost impossible to stand up in the stirrups when your legs are straight to start with.

RACING

An American jockey named Tod Sloan changed the style of race-riding forever in the 1800s. Before he came to England to ride in races, jockeys rode with long stirrups. Tod introduced the very short stirrup leather. He was laughed at and called a "monkey on a stick." Despite this, his technique was soon copied by jockeys everywhere.

Did you know?

The Spanish Riding School in Vienna trains its horses in what is called the classic style of horsemanship. The beautiful white Lipizzaner stallions are taught High School movements (right). The Spanish Riding School travels all over the world giving demonstrations, which are well worth a visit. The horses are very supple, calm, and obedient, and wonderfully in tune with their talented riders.

Jumping

Everyone today is taught the forward seat when jumping. This lets the hands follow the movement of the horse and keeps the rider's weight evenly distributed. This method is one hundred years old. It dates back to the teachings of an Italian cavalry officer, Federico Caprilli. Before that, riders leaned forward on takeoff and back on landing.

Western

With a deep seat and straight legs, cowboys found that they could ride for many miles and not get too tired. Provided that the saddle fits properly, this style is kind to the horse, too. Western horses are trained to respond to the reins touching the neck. A touch on the right side makes the horse turn left and vice versa.

Sidesaddle

Sidesaddle riding is considered a very elegant riding style. In the past it was the only acceptable way for a lady to ride. The "leaping head," the downturned horn fitted below the upward horn on the saddle, makes it possible for sidesaddle riders to have a firm seat, jump, and gallop safely.

Medieval knights

The cavalry was an important part of the army, and all officers were mounted. They rode with long stirrups, straight legs, and their feet forward. This style looks similar to that of Western riders. The armor worn by the military horsemen of northern Europe was so bulky that only very strong horses could carry them. Some needed cranes to lift them onto their horses. If a soldier fell off, he was not able to get on again.

Horses in fiction

Stories about horses have been popular for many years, from the classics of earlier days to the pony books of today. Some fictional horses live forever, continuing to delight each generation of readers. Some of them are listed here.

Tuesday
Before I had Oscar, I spent most of my time reading. I thought I'd read all the horse books ever written! But Oscar takes up so much of my day, reading has moved into second place. Now, most of my books are practical ones on pony care.

SILVER

This horse was almost certainly the first to become famous through radio and television. He is a handsome gray who belongs to the Lone Ranger. The Lone Ranger is a masked man who rides anonymously through the Wild West, solving crimes and restoring law and order wherever he goes.

FLICKA

Flicka is the horse heroine of *My Friend Flicka*, a book written by Mary O'Hara about the love of a boy for his horse. The setting is a ranch in Wyoming, and the book gives a vivid picture of domesticating and training wild horses in the West just before World War II. The picture (left) is from the movie based on the book. The book is no longer in print, but it can be found in second-hand bookstores.

BLACK BEAUTY

A young writer, Anna Sewell, hated seeing carriage horses in bearing reins. These are straps that forced horses to carry their heads at an uncomfortable angle. She wrote a book about the life of a carriage horse, *Black Beauty*. She included other characters, such as Merrylegs and Ginger. The book is a classic and led to the prohibition of bearing reins in the U.K.

THE RED PONY

The Red Pony is a short story by John Steinbeck. The pony, which belongs to a young boy, gets sick and dies. The boy blames his father for the pony's death, but the two of them struggle to build a new relationship. In 1949, the story, which does finally have a happy ending, was made into a prize-winning film.

Afternoon—Annabel and I go to our local library, but we can't always find the books we want to read. So Annabel said why don't we get together with friends at the stable and form our own book-lending group. I thought that was a brilliant idea. So that's what we've done. There are loads of books I haven't read yet.

ROSINANTE

This horse is an example of beauty being in the eye of the beholder. Rosinante is an ugly old nag who generally fails in anything he is asked to do. But to his owner, Don Quixote, a self-styled knight, he is a status symbol and the best horse in the world. *Don Quixote* was written by Miguel de Cervantes in the 1600s and is a classic of European literature.

Horses in history

Just as there are famous people in history, so there are some horses whose names will never be forgotten. A few are remembered because their owners were great men, but others—mostly racehorses—are legends in their own right.

Saturday
What do you think Oscar would have to do to go down in history? He's certainly not a charger or a racehorse. But he's a really cool pony and I'm lucky to have him. He's going down in my history, anyway.

BUCEPHALUS

Bucephalus belonged to Alexander the Great. He was thought to be unridable until Alexander realized that the horse was frightened of his own shadow. By turning Bucephalus toward the sun, Alexander could mount him. Alexander became a powerful warrior and rode Bucephalus in all his campaigns.

COPENHAGEN

Copenhagen, a chestnut, was a grandson of the racehorse Eclipse. He was much loved by his owner, the Duke of Wellington. He accompanied the "Iron Duke" through many of his battles, including the victory over Napoleon at Waterloo.

CHALK HORSES

Figures of horses have been carved into the chalk downland of Southern England for thousands of years. The oldest chalk horse is at Uffington, Oxfordshire, and is thought to be 3,000 years old. A new one may be carved in Kent, near the entrance to the Channel Tunnel between England and France.

ECLIPSE

Possibly the greatest racehorse that has ever lived, Eclipse was born in 1764 during an eclipse of the sun. He never lost a race. His owner once predicted the result of a race as "Eclipse first and the rest nowhere." A chestnut horse, Eclipse sired (fathered) 335 winners after finishing his racing career. He died, aged 25, in 1789.

RED RUM

Red Rum won the Grand National, one of the hardest steeplechases in the world, no fewer than three times. His first win, in 1973, broke the course record. He completed the four-and-a-half-mile course, over 30 jumps, in 9 minutes 1.9 seconds.

I'm making a scrapbook about Oscar and me. I keep a record of everything we do together and call it "The History of Oscar."

SECRETARIAT

In 1970, Secretariat, one of the most famous American racehorses, was born in Virginia. In his career, he won the U.S. Triple Crown—the Kentucky Derby, the Belmont Stakes, and the Preakness Stakes. He completed the Kentucky Derby in the fastest time ever and won the Belmont Stakes by 31 lengths!

Q When is a horse not a horse?

A Apart from a clothes horse, the answer is the Trojan Horse. In Greek mythology, the Greeks were besieging the city of Troy but could not break the Trojans' resistance. Then they built a huge wooden horse, in which they hid dozens of warriors. They gave it to the Trojans as a gift, which the Trojans accepted. Once inside the city, warriors poured out of the horse and captured Troy.

In the beginning

Early horses looked nothing like the horses of today. It took 50 million years of evolution for the cat-sized creature that lived in the Northern Hemisphere to become the handsome, elegant horse we all admire now. Only in the last 5,000 years has the horse been ridden by man.

HYRACOTHERIUM

Also known as Eohippus ("Dawn Horse"), Hyracotherium was a funny little creature. It had four toes on its front feet and three toes on the back. From all the fossilized bones found in the southern U.S., it seems likely that it originated on the American continent.

Hyracotherium

MESOHIPPUS

The next stage in the evolution was the Mesohippus. It had a similar bone structure to the Hyracotherium, but was bigger. Still a small creature, it was beginning to emerge from the forest to graze on the plains. Its feet were still multitoed, but the outer toes were less pronounced. Its weight was carried on the central toe.

Mesohippus

INTO DANGER

The little prehistoric horses, coming out of the safety of the forest, were able to run quite fast. This was their way of avoiding danger. But they were no match for predatory birds. These creatures, with their sharp eyesight, could easily spot the tiny horses, in spite of their striped camouflage. Many horses ended up as a tasty morsel.

Q How big were the first horses?

A They were very small. Hyracotherium was not much bigger than a domestic cat. Certainly too small for a human to ride, even if early man had been in existence at the time. Throughout the millions of years of evolution, horses got bigger and stronger.

HOTBLOODS AND COLDBLOODS

As the horse evolved, two types emerged. In the northern countries, the coldbloods were predominant. They developed into the heavy horses of today, powerfully built, strong creatures. They could be trained to pull a plow or wagon or to carry a man in a full suit of armor. Farther south were the hotbloods, horses like the desert Arabian. These were lighter in build but very hardy and tough. Many of today's horses are crosses between the two types and are known as warmbloods.

EQUUS

This is the true horse, common ancestor of all our present-day horses. It was a single-toed mammal standing about 13 hands high (52 inches). Equus had a large head, heavy neck, faint stripes on its fore and hindquarters, and possibly a dorsal stripe along its backbone. Its mane was short and stood up like a shaving brush.

Merichippus

Equus

MERICHIPPUS

Merichippus was more recognizable as a horse. The outer toes had almost disappeared and the central toe was broadening into a hoof. This was a creature of the plains, no longer feeding on trees but capable of eating grass. Its natural defense was to run away. In spite of the vast prairies of America, horses disappeared from the American continent. They did not return for several thousand years, until brought back by the conquistadors in the 1500s.

Morning
I had a nightmare last night.
I dreamed that I was a
Dawn Horse living in a
prehistoric world. I was
being chased by a caveman.
I was so glad to wake up!

Early times

Most of the great horse people of the olden days, between 2000 and 1000 B.C., lived in or roamed the Middle East. Some used horses for riding or as pack animals; others harnessed them to chariots. Either way, the horse was a symbol indicating a great chieftain or warrior.

Hun

SCYTHIANS

These people flourished in the Altai Mountains of Central Asia around 1500 B.C. The frozen tombs of Scythian chieftains and their horses were discovered in the 1920s. They revealed that the horses were fed on grain and their tack consisted of lavishly decorated felt saddle pads. The bridles were crowned by reindeer headdresses.

EASTERN HORSEMEN

Most tribes of Central Asia were nomadic, moving about in pursuit of food supplies. The tribesmen were superb horsemen. The Huns were so dedicated to their steeds that they dismounted only to sleep. The Chinese fought and traded with the Huns. They also found that horses flourished in the damp lowlands of China, so they established vast breeding centers.

EGYPTIANS

The Egyptians are believed to have adapted the use of horses when they were introduced into Egypt by the nomadic Hyksos tribe. They drew two-wheeled chariots and were almost certainly used by the Egyptian army. Other peoples of the Near East and North Africa were excellent horsemen, including the Babylonians and Assyrians.

ROMANS

Roman armies generally fought on foot but Roman generals, wishing to make an impression, would enter a captured town or city on horseback. Horses were also used to draw racing chariots and parade in ceremonies. Only in the later part of the Roman Empire did the cavalry come into widespread use.

GREEKS

Greek horsemanship is well known because of the literature that has survived from ancient times. Best known of the ancient Greek equine writers is Xenophon. He was a general who wrote in detail describing the way horses should be trained and cared for. Many of his ideas are still valid today although saddles and stirrups had not been invented—the Greeks always rode bareback.

Q What about mythical horses?

A Best known of legendary horses is Pegasus, the winged horse of Greek mythology. He is said to have sprung from the blood of Medusa and was caught with the help of a magic bridle made of gold. His rider, Bellerophon, tried to take Pegasus to heaven. But this angered Zeus, the chief of the gods, and he sent a fly to sting Pegasus. Bellerophon fell to earth, but Pegasus flew on and became a constellation in the night sky. Another mythical creature was the centaur, half man, half horse. The centaur Chiron survives in the sky as the constellation Sagittarius.

Afternoon
I'm glad we live in the 21st century. I wouldn't have wanted to ride without stirrups like they did in ancient times. Annabel and I tried riding without stirrups for an hour and it was so tiring. It's amazing how much support you get from them.

Heavy horses

In their time, the size and strength of heavy horses made them the most important of the horse breeds, and even today they are impressive. But in many places they no longer have a role, and only careful conservation will prevent them from dying out.

OLD AMERICAN HORSES
The most versatile all-purpose horse in America is the Morgan. It is a combination of the best qualities of both draft and riding horses. It is powerful, intelligent, and has great stamina.

PLOWING WITH HORSES
Until 50 years ago, heavy horses were used for farmwork throughout the Western world. They are still used in some countries. These massive but willing animals were the engines of agriculture. They can pull plows and threshing machines, and work tirelessly all day.

JOUSTING
A man in full armor is very heavy, and the horse had to be immensely strong to carry him. During the Age of Chivalry, tournaments became popular. Knights competed against each other, trying to knock each other off their horses. The two riders used their lances as battering rams.

TODAY'S CAVALRY

Heavy horses are no longer used by the cavalry, which do not need weight-carriers. The cavalry has no role in modern warfare, but it is still an impressive sight when taking part in state ceremonies. The annual Trooping of the Color on Horseguards Parade in London is a spectacular sight.

DRAY HORSES

In Britain, several big breweries still use heavy horses to pull their drays. It is not unusual to see beer barrels being unloaded outside a pub (bar), while the pair of shire horses harnessed to the dray enjoy their lunch

from nosebags. Classes for tradesmen's drays are usually held at agricultural shows. They parade around the arena giving a magnificent display.

Suffolk Punch
England

Clydesdale
Scotland

Dutch Draft
Holland

HEAVY HORSES TODAY

Efforts are now being made to conserve breeds that might otherwise die out. The Suffolk Punch, a British breed that is always chestnut and has no feathers (longer hair) on its legs, is the most endangered. Special societies support the preservation of working breeds around the world.

The messenger

The speed and stamina of the horse made them the perfect means for carrying messages, and for many centuries, they served as the fastest messengers. From 5th-century Persia, through 13th-century Mongolia, to 19th-century America, horses, ridden in shifts, carried news across the world.

Mom has made me two saddlebags so that Annabel and I can take something to eat when we go off on a long ride.

THE PONY EXPRESS

The Pony Express was a rapid mail service between the central U.S. and California. In 1860, a private company established 190 stations along the 2,000-mile route between St. Joseph, Missouri, and Sacramento, California. They bought 500 fast horses, and recruited 120 riders to carry saddlebags of messages across the Great Plains, over two towering mountain ranges, and through the vast badlands of Utah and Nevada. The first relay arrived in just over ten days, and later deliveries were made in only seven.

Sacramento

Salt Lake City

St. Joseph

St. Louis

THE AMERICAN STAGECOACH

In the American west in the late 1800s, horse-drawn stagecoaches traveled between widely separated towns, carrying valuable cargo as well as passengers. Bands of outlaws often waylaid a stagecoach, taking its strongbox full of gold and silver and robbing passengers of any valuables. Local residents often tried to catch the robbers on horseback.

PAUL REVERE

Paul Revere was one of several horsemen who slipped out of Boston on the night of April 18, 1775, to warn outlying towns that British troops were on the march against the Massachusetts colonists. The next morning, the British met strong resistance at Lexington and Concord in battles that marked the beginning of the American Revolution.

DELIVERING NEWS

Most long-distance riders use relays of horses and, in this way, manage to cover great distances in a very short time. The Mongol Post in the 1200s routinely traveled 125 mi in one day; the fastest ride they recorded was 210 mi. In the Middle Ages, heralds (above) relayed important news to their king. These knights had distinctive coats of arms that were used to identify them in battle.

ROYAL MAIL COACHES

The Royal Mail coaches carried the mail from London to different places in the British Isles. The coaches were usually pulled by four horses, which would be changed at regular intervals. The great boast of the coach drivers was that they would always get through, no matter what snowstorms or other terrible conditions they came across on the way, and that they were always on schedule. Passengers could also travel on the coaches.

Thursday
It must have been exciting to be a Pony Express rider, except that it was dangerous and scary. But taking the mail and dashing off into hostile country must have been fantastic. No wonder there were so many willing riders.

Tack through the ages

Various methods of controling the horse have been tried since ancient times. Some of them aren't very different from those used today. Saddles were a later development than bits, but it was the invention of the stirrup that transformed riding. Stirrups gave riders the chance to attain a balanced seat and to ride in harmony with their horse.

11 am—I can't imagine using a bridle without a bit. I think it would feel strange. Still, my instructor at the stable says that in the right hands, a bitless bridle is just as effective as a snaffle bridle. I don't think Oscar would mind what I use— he thinks he looks gorgeous in anything.

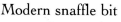

THE BITLESS BRIDLE

The hackamore, or bitless, bridle is widely used but always with care. It acts on the nose and, in rough hands, can easily cut off a horse's air supply. The cowboys of South America, the gauchos, usually use a form of bitless bridle knotted under the chin. They often use a single rein, but their horsemanship is superb.

EARLY BITS

The snaffle bit was first used by Iron Age Celts, originally as a straight-bar snaffle and then with a joint. The early jointed snaffle was almost exactly the same as the snaffle bit of today. Snaffle bits act on the tongue and the corners of the horse's mouth and cause it to raise its head.

Celtic snaffle bit

Modern snaffle bit

THE MIDDLE AGES

In the Middle Ages, bits were very elaborate. The shanks were decorated and usually very long. The mouthpiece had a high central port, or hump. When pressure was applied to the reins, the bit acted on both the bars and roof of the mouth. This caused the horse to bend heavily at its poll. Knights preferred to use curb bits.

shank

Medieval curb bit

HOW A MODERN CURB WORKS

The modern curb bit works in exactly the same way as the medieval curb. But the modern shanks are shorter and the mouthpiece is less severe. Pressure on the lower rein causes the bit to press on the bars of the mouth. It causes the curb chain to tighten in the chin groove, and the headpiece to press on the poll. Instinctively the horse will lower its head, bend at the poll, and flex its jaw. The curb bit can be combined with a snaffle bit to form a double bridle.

Q When were stirrups invented?

A Stirrups were developed by the Huns in the 400s A.D. They first learned to make a saddle with a tree (frame) and then attached stirrups to the framework of the saddle. The Huns were archers and galloped alongside their enemies, shooting at them over their shoulders. Stirrups let them do this without losing their balance. Modern-day mounted games players rely on stirrups for balance in the same way.

Roman saddle

Working with horses

If you love riding and horses, it is not surprising that you would like to go on being with horses. You may choose to go on riding in your leisure time, on weekends, or in vacations. Or you may, like many others before you, decide to work with horses full time.

TEACHING

Firstly, you need to be a proficient rider. Secondly, it's important that you enjoy people as well as horses. Today, instructors have formal qualifications, which you should study for if you want to teach. The American Riding Instructors Association has a course of examinations that you can take to become a riding instructor.

Did you know?

To become a farrier you must enroll on a two-week basic farrier course where you learn to make shoes, basic trimming, and shoeing techniques. Or you can enroll on longer courses that include therapeutic and corrective shoeing. There are a number of farriery schools in the U.S. Following this, you can take up an apprenticeship with a "Journeyman Farrier." Here you will gain a lot of experience until you are ready to try it alone.

Afternoon—Oscar really enjoys lots of company, especially with people. I think he would like to have a job where he could be with humans. He would work on his laptop when he was traveling on the train to his office each day. Imagine that?!

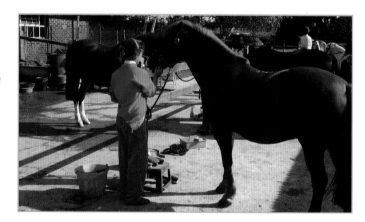

BARN WORKER/STABLE HELP

A barn worker's job can be very rewarding although it is hard work and the pay is quite poor. You will be expected to feed the horses, clean the stalls, repair fencing, help out when the farrier comes, and generally keep the barn clean and tidy.

RACING

Jockeys are very small and light. To be an apprentice jockey, you must not be heavier than 110 pounds (50 kg). Apprenticeships can be had with stables all over the world. Apprentices are trained in horse handling, grooming, hoof care, horse health, feeding, stable skills, and trackwork riding. If you are too heavy to become a jockey, you could consider becoming a barn worker at a racing stable.

BARN MANAGER

Barn managers are responsible for the day-to-day running of the barn and also for the barn workers and the horses. Although a degree isn't essential, it is helpful to have a degree in Equine Studies or Equine Management. This will ensure you have all the necessary skills, such as equine business knowledge, communications skills, riding, and horsecare skills.

Tuesday

I think it would be good fun to be a barn manager. Just think, you'd get to spend every day with loads of different horses. Mom says it's hard work and a really responsible job, but I reckon I could do it. I'll just have to get some more practical horsecare skills and then do a training course. How hard can it be?! I think it would be worth it.

Q What about helping out with riding for the handicapped?

A Every year around 20,000 people volunteer to help out at North American Riding for the Handicapped Association (NARHA) centers. If you have no horsemanship experience, you will need to be over 14 years old. If you are younger and have some experience, it is likely that you'll be accepted. Volunteers help by leading the horse, sidewalking (walking alongside the horse to help support the rider), grooming, tacking up horses, cooling off horses, cleaning tack, helping with fundraisers, and assisting with administrative duties.

Quiz time

How much do you know about the world of horses? Here is a chance for you and your friends to test your knowledge.

1 Where do the "golden" horses come from?

2 What name is given to the wild horses of North America?

3 Name two of the contests in a young riders' rodeo.

4 Who was the first jockey to ride with very short stirrups?

5 Where would you find the Spanish riding school?

6 Who wrote *Black Beauty?*

7 What was the name of the Duke of Wellington's horse?

8 How many toes did the "dawn horse" (hyracotherium or eohippus) have on its front feet and how many on the back?

9 What heavy horse comes from Scotland?

10 What are the people who look after racehorses in a racing stable known as?

Useful addresses

USA Pony Clubs
4041 Iron Works
  Parkway
Lexington
KY 40511-8462
www.ponyclub.org
Tel: (859) 254-7669

USA Equestrian, Inc.
4047 Iron Works
  Parkway
Lexington
KY 40511-8463
www.equestrian.org
Tel: (859) 254-2476

11 am—Annabel and I did a quiz on Saturday. Some of the questions were on the history of horses, and we got every one right. Cool!

Answers

1 Russia 2 Mustangs 3 Bronco riding, bareback riding, calf roping, steer wrestling, and goat tying 4 Tod Sloan 5 Vienna, Austria 6 Anna Sewell 7 Copenhagen 8 Four on the front, three on the back 9 Clydesdale 10 Barn workers/stable help

Glossary

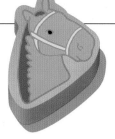

bit
A metal bar attached to the reins that fits in the pony's mouth.

chalk horse
A horse shape that is carved into the side of a chalk hill.

cowboy
A person on horseback who drives cattle across many miles of plains.

dorsal stripe
A stripe of dark hair that runs along the back of a horse from the mane to the tail.

dray
A heavy cart that is pulled by horses. Drays are used to carry barrels of beer in the U.K.

gaucho
A South American cowboy.

groom
A person who looks after a horse.

hackamore
A bridle that has no bit. The horse is controlled by pressure exerted on its nose.

hands
Horses and ponies are measured in hands. One hand is equal to 4 inches (10 cm).

jousting
A tournament in the Middle Ages where knights fought with lances.

lance
A long pole that was carried by knights in jousting competitions. It was used for knocking the opponent off the horse.

livery
The name given to the practice of keeping a pony at a stable that isn't your own. You pay a fee to the owner of the stable.

mustang
A wild horse of North America.

neck-reining
Guiding a horse with only one hand on the reins.

pacer
Horse with an artificial gait, in which both legs on one side move forward at the same time.

rodeo
A competition in which cowboys display their riding and cattle-roping skills.

steeplechasing
A horse race that is run over jumps.

steer
A young bull or ox.

sulky
A two-wheeled, lightweight cart used for racing.

trail riding
Exploring the countryside on horseback.

wild horses
Horses that are untamed and live in the wild.

yearling
A horse that is between one and two years old.

Index

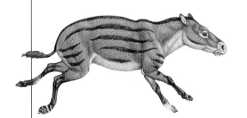

Photo credits

Abbreviations: l-left, r-right, b-bottom, t-top, c-center, m-middle
Front cover, 1, 3b, 7ml, 9ml, 13tl, 13c, 21ml, 22c, 25tr, 30c, 31 both—Corel. Back cover, 5ml, 9tr, 16br, 23tl, 28br, 29ml, 30ml—Select Pictures. 2b, 4tr, 5tl, 5mt, 8bm, 9br, 10tl, 12c, 23ml, 23br, 27 both, 29tl, 29br—Horsepix. 4c, 5br, 6 both, 7mr, 10c, 10br, 11tl, 11br, 12br, 13bl, 17ml, 19tl, 25c, 28ml—Kit Houghton Photography. 11ct—Kelly-Mooney Photography/CORBIS. 11ml—Jerry Cooke/CORBIS. 12tr—Leonard de Selva/CORBIS. 14-15 all — The Kobal Collection. 16c—Brian Hunter Smart. 17tr, 17mr—Bettmann/CORBIS. 22mr—Corbis Royalty Free. 25tr—Photodisc.